Graduating from QuickBooks:
Enter a New Program
with SAP Business One

Graduating from QuickBooks:

Enter a New Program with SAP Business One

Table of Contents

Table of Contents

Introduction: Moving Your Business To The Next Stage of Growth 3

Graduate 1: Industry-Leading IT Company Suffering From Information Silos 4

Lack of Integration with Other Applications 4

Inaccessible Business Data 4

Poor System Performance 4

The ERP Solution To Fast Growth 5

Graduate 2: Multinational Distribution Company Challenged to Manage Inventory Effectively 6

Limited Inventory Management 6

Unable to Interface with Other Applications 6

Lack of Real-Time Reporting 6

The ERP Solution To Inventory Management 7

Graduate 3: Benefits Solution Provider, Financial Compliance Challenges 8

Limited Financial Reporting 8

Unable to Make Real-Time Decisions 8

Lack of Accounting Compliance 8

The ERP Solution To Financial Compliance 9

The Program: SAP Business One; Bringing Together All Business Faculties Under One Roof 10

QuickBooks vs. SAP Business One Cheat Sheet 11

Introduction

Moving Your Business To The Next Stage of Growth

Moving Your Business To The Next Stage of Growth

As the owner of a small to midsized enterprise (SME), you've watched your business grow over the years. From the first day of operations, all you needed was a simple accounting package like Intuit's QuickBooks; a system that would keep you on track with payroll, bookkeeping, sales and expenses, while providing you with the basics to measure your company's performance. As your business grew, milestones were reached; from opening your first new sales office or warehouse, to product go-lives and expanding into new markets. At this point, you are likely a QuickBooks pro, ready to graduate at the top of your class and with a strong foundation of knowledge needed to move your business further.

However as your business moves beyond the entry level, you have started to encounter limitations that prevent you from automating key processes, obtaining real-time information, and integrating critical business applications. Trying to meet your business' needs with the narrow range of features in QuickBooks may be causing inefficiencies and slowing your business' growth. While QuickBooks helped your business get up and running, it is now falling behind, unable to keep up with your business needs. Having achieved a level of complexity and sophistication - you are ready to graduate from QuickBooks.

If you are to continue to be successful, you will need an integrated system that will provide complete operational visibility and the scalability necessary to support your growth well into the future. By moving into an integrated Enterprise Resource Planning (ERP) solution, you open the door to functionality you need to continue to operate your business efficiently and take advantage of new opportunities. If your business is planning on growing its human resources past 30 users, or has achieved sales greater than 2 million annual, now is the time to prepare for your business' future.

Graduating QuickBooks: Enter a New Program with SAP Business One is written with fast-growing business like yours in mind. Presenting three different business scenarios, the eBook describes common challenges facing companies that have achieved a level of business complexity that QuickBooks is unable to support. Continue reading to find out how an integrated ERP solution can provide your business with the tools necessary to overcome these challenges and support your business in the next stage of growth.

Graduate 1

Industry-Leading IT Company Suffering From Information Silos

Graduate 1: Industry-Leading IT Company Suffering From Information Silos

An industry-leading IT solutions provider that specializes in network security and related products has built a successful business over the past 12 years; assisting buyers at each stage of their IT decision-making process through product fulfillment and post-sales support. By consistently meeting its customers' expectations, the company had experienced tremendous business growth – earning recognition on the prestigious Inc. 5000 list, processing more than 2,500 customer orders a month.

Until now, the company had supported its operations with QuickBooks, however as the product lineup expanded, it became harder to keep up with demand. The biggest issue for this fast-growing SME was not having full visibility into their orders and overall operations. They started using additional applications to access this key information, only to discover Quickbooks' limitations in integrating with other applications.

It was at this stage of growth when the successful company realized that their business had reached a higher level of performance, and it was time to evaluate the next step in business management software – a fully integrated ERP solution.

QuickBooks Integration Performance Report Card

Integrates with other applications	✘
Provides real-time reporting for improved visibility	✘
Supports over 30 users to accommodate for scalability	✘
Supports multiple warehouses and inventory control	✘
API customizability	✘

EVALUATION:

QuickBooks does not provide visibility of operations needed for this business to make better decisions and meet growth requirements.

Key Business Challenges with QuickBooks:

1. Lack of Integration with Other Applications

Although the company had been using QuickBooks since its inception, the closed system prevented extending the limited customer relationship management (CRM) functionality of the application.

The limited API resulted in the company manually integrating with separate applications which resulted in information silos.

2. Inaccessible Business Data

The company was running its business with 3 separate applications that did not communicate with each other. This made accessing information stored in disparate location difficult to access.

QuickBooks' limited reporting did not provide the company with access to key information it needed to make business decisions. Lacking key information about its growing customer base, the company knew that without a single integrated solution, it would not be able to support its growth, or the needs of its customers.

3. Poor System Performance

With over 20 users and processing 2,500 orders per month, the IT company's system slowed to a crawl. As an IT solutions provider, its extensive product line of 85 items translated into hundreds of thousands of product numbers. While the company does not carry that many parts in stock, the parts were still required to be entered into the system to create quotes and customer orders.

With 30% year over year growth, the company was encroaching on the maximum number of users to which they could provide licenses. Additionally, the number of products they were loading into the system was resulting in very slow performance.

Graduate 1

The ERP Solution To Fast Growth

The ERP Solution To Fast Growth

Upon realizing that the company needed to graduate from QuickBooks, the decision was made to move to search for a more comprehensive application that would enable them to achieve their goals.

With SAP Business One, growing SMEs like the IT solution provider are able to adapt the application to meet their changing needs through various core modules or by integrating with other systems using intuitive technologies.

Key Business Benefits with an ERP solution

1. Integration

By moving from QuickBooks to SAP Business One, the company is now able to integrate its business backend with its website, new customers and web orders are imported directly into the system via the SAP Business One API.

Now whenever the company needs to quote or sell new products, they can import vendor or distributor's data into their system automatically and the information is then made available to the company's sales people to quote directly from SAP Business One.

2. Visibility

SAP Business One has given the company better visibility and control over its licensing which is the core of its business. Management can now see all open items, which orders have yet to be processed, and then report on that information.

Additionally, SAP Business One has given them greater control over the movement of products moving out from their warehouse or the returns coming back from customers.

3. Performance

Since moving from QuickBooks, the company has been able handle a large volume of transactions through SAP Business One.

While there is a limit to the number of product IDS entered into QuickBooks before system performance is affected, ERP does not. With SAP Business One, the company can scale its operations or product offering without adversely affecting system performance.

Graduate 2

Multinational Distribution Company Challenged to Manage Inventory Effectively

Graduate 2: Multinational Distribution Company Challenged to Manage Inventory Effectively

Growing SMEs understand the central role that inventory management plays in their business' success. Take for instance a growing business in the cinema supplies industry; as an industry pioneer, the company's success was built on its commitment to delivering comprehensive cinema solutions to its customers. Consistently acknowledged by industry associations for its growth, the company had begun planning to expand into emerging markets in South America, which required maintaining a larger volume of materials to meet demand.

However, with the installation of 600 digital projection systems installed in over 15 countries worldwide, the company was quickly outpacing QuickBooks' ability to support the SMEs' inventory information needs. With the company's plan to continue expanding into overseas markets well underway, the company began searching for a new business management solution that would help minimize its inventory holding costs.

QuickBooks Inventory Performance Report Card

Lot, bin and warehouse management	✔
LIFO and FIFO inventory methods	✖
Landed cost ability to ensure visibility of container shipments oversees and allocate inventory en route to customers	✖
Vendor performance tracking	✖
Production and material requirements planning	✖

EVALUATION:

QuickBooks does not have inventory management for this business without the manual add-ons.

Key Business Challenges with QuickBooks:

1. Limited Inventory Management

Inventory management in QuickBooks is limited and it is not possible for the supplier to specifically manage the materials side of manufacturing.

This posed as a problem since they needed the flexibility to do light manufacturing but QuickBooks could not provide them with current information about their inventory to minimize holding costs.

2. Unable to Interface with Other Applications

For the cinema equipment supplier another key challenge was that QuickBooks did not provide the ability to integrate with other applications.

Since QuickBooks is limited to tracking lead to shipment and does not have sales order/purchase order, bill of materials or work assemblies, the company was required to add support for these processes through manual integration of third party applications.

3. Lack of Real-Time Reporting

With overseas expansion into emerging markets on the horizon, key management personnel and decision makers for the cinema supplier are often traveling away from corporate offices.

Away from a computer terminal, the company did not have access to real-time information needed to make important business decisions. The company faced lost time due to inefficiencies and lack of business intelligence while traveling.

Graduate 2

The ERP Solution To Inventory Management

The ERP Solution To Inventory Management

SAP Business One provides accurate information about inbound and outbound shipments, inventory and item location. Now the cinema equipment solutions supplier can value inventory using standard costing, moving average, FIFO, and other methods; monitor stock levels; and track transfers in real time.

Running run real-time inventory updates and availability checks and manage standard and special pricing is also possible. The cinema solutions provider now has the ability to continue providing great customer service with volume, cash, and customer discounts and run reports that reveal their impact on the company's bottom line.

Key Business Benefits with an ERP Solution

1. Inventory Management

Since the supplier does not hold inventory and instead purchases on an order basis, they can take advantage of the SAP Business One procurement confirmation wizard. This feature automatically creates purchase quotations for orders by confirming the information from one or more sales orders.

At a moment's notice, the company can see order status on a much deeper level of detail in addition to measuring the time span before an order is shipped out.

2. Interfacing with Other Applications

SAP Business One enables companies that run multiple specialized applications to integrate seamlessly with the system.

The supplier is able to interface with other systems including an eCommerce system that links directly to the customer account. When the lifespan of a particular product reaches its end, the system automatically creates an order for a replacement part for the customer for greater customer service.

3. Efficient Reporting

By moving to SAP Business One, the company is now able to make real-time decisions about its inventory.

Now, when a valued customer places an order for supplies on credit, a senior manager can approve the transaction even while traveling via a mobile phone app. This results in improved efficiency with orders being placed much faster.

Graduate 3

Benefits Solution Provider Facing Financial Compliance Challenges

Graduate 3: Benefits Solution Provider

Facing Financial Compliance Challenges

Strong client relationships are built on trust; a statement that holds particular significance for one fast-growing employee benefits solution provider in the U.S. As an industry leader, the company built its success on providing reliable service and comprehensive employee benefit solutions to over twenty trusts; maintaining complete financials for its clients in addition to its own business.

However as the company continued to grow, managing relationships between its clients and insurance providers started to become a challenge. With a dense volume of transactions, the company realized that its business had out-complexed QuickBooks' functionality. Determined to improve its financial performance and continue to provide reliable services, the company realized that it would have to find a business management solution that would enable them to support a growing number of financial transactions while achieving industry compliance.

**QuickBooks
Financial Performance
Report Card**

GAAP compliant to meet auditing requirements	✔
Divisional/departmental accounting	✖
Sales tax by line item	✖
Multidimensional General Ledger account structure	✖

EVALUATION:

QuickBooks does not enable businesses to meet industry standards for accounting compliance.

Key Business Challenges with QuickBooks:

1. Limited Financial Reporting

Since QuickBooks does not integrate with other systems, the company would typically accumulate journal entries in one system and then create a manual journal entry in QuickBooks with the same dollar amount - without any justification for matching a specific transaction back to the balance sheet.

This is an issue for accounts such as Goods Received Not Invoiced (GRNI) where businesses are required to keep a constant reconciliation of what they have currently on the shelf.

2. Unable to Make Real-Time Decisions

With QuickBooks, the benefits provider was required to manually post journal entries at the end of each month to create a balance sheet. This process was so laborious that it was not feasible to obtain a snapshot of the company's performance mid-month against its predefined goals without manually recreating all of the journal entries.

This prevented the company from making real-time operation changes to help stay on target to meet its monthly goals.

3. Lack of Accounting Compliance

Like many growing businesses, the primary driver to move to a new business management system was a lack of accounting control – QuickBooks is not SOC or GAAP compliant.

This means that QuickBooks does not offer a way to prevent the modification, or deletion of journal entries. Compliance is critical for growing businesses that are expanding operations and need to report to an increasing number of stakeholders or that need to meet the requirements of an auditing process.

Graduate 3

The ERP Solution To Financial Compliance

The ERP Solution To Financial Compliance

SAP Business One provides a complete set of tools to help manage and streamline the financial operations.of the benefits solution provider. It automates everyday accounting tasks such as maintaining ledger and journal entries, supporting tax calculations, and enabling multi-currency transactions.

Key Business Benefits with an ERP Solution

1. Financial Reporting

With SAP Business One, all of the company's business operations are now consolidated into the one application. This means that it is no longer required to manually post journal entries from one application. This to their business management solution.

The company can now get access to SAP Business One extensive metrics for individual transactions that they could not have obtained with a manual QuickBooks integration.

2. Real-time Decision Making

SAP Business One also provides the Company with the ability to obtain business insight through real-time reporting at a moment's notice. The ability to print out financial reports such as a profit and loss statement or a balance sheet helps management determine whether or not the company is reaching their goals or if they are in need of adjustment.

This helps the company with decision making but, also makes it possible to track accounts receivable that were not easily accessible with manual, one-time journal entries.

3. Accounting Compliance

Since the company moved to the new system, they are now able to integrate SAP Business One with their proprietary system while maintaining compliance.

In compliant applications like SAP Business One, users are prevented from modifying journal entries in isolation. Since SAP Business One meets industry compliance such as GAAP and SOC compliance, users will have to reverse journal entries then repost them which is the compliant way to make changes to journal entries.

SAP Business One

Bringing Together All Business Faculties Under One Roof

SAP Business One: Bringing Together All Business Faculties Under One Roof

SAP Business One is a single, integrated solution that provides clear visibility into your entire business and complete control over every aspect of your operations. The three graduates of QuickBooks in the previous scenarios were all trying to make a solution fit that they had clearly outgrown. QuickBooks was unable to support their business' growth past 30 users, inventory levels over 30,000 items, or annual revenues of more than 2 million. Unable to automate key business processes, integrate with other critical applications, or obtain visibility across their

Why Your Business Is Ready to Graduate from QuickBooks

SAP Business One captures all critical business information for immediate access and use company-wide. Unlike accounting packages and spreadsheets, it delivers what you need to manage your business. Above and beyond the areas covered in the three scenarios, SAP Business One provides comprehensive support for:

- Accounting and finance
- Sales and customer management
- Purchasing and operations
- Inventory and distribution
- Reporting and administration

If your business is experiencing similar challenges with QuickBooks as the businesses described in the above scenarios then you ready to graduate from QuickBooks.

Moving to a single system that can not only manage your accounting, sales, inventory, and reporting needs but also give you real-time access to business intelligence for better decision-making, which is critical for growing businesses. Graduate from QuickBooks and take the next step with an ERP solution for your fast-growing business. To see what functionality your business could be taking advantage of, continue reading the QuickBooks vs. SAP Business One Cheat Sheet.

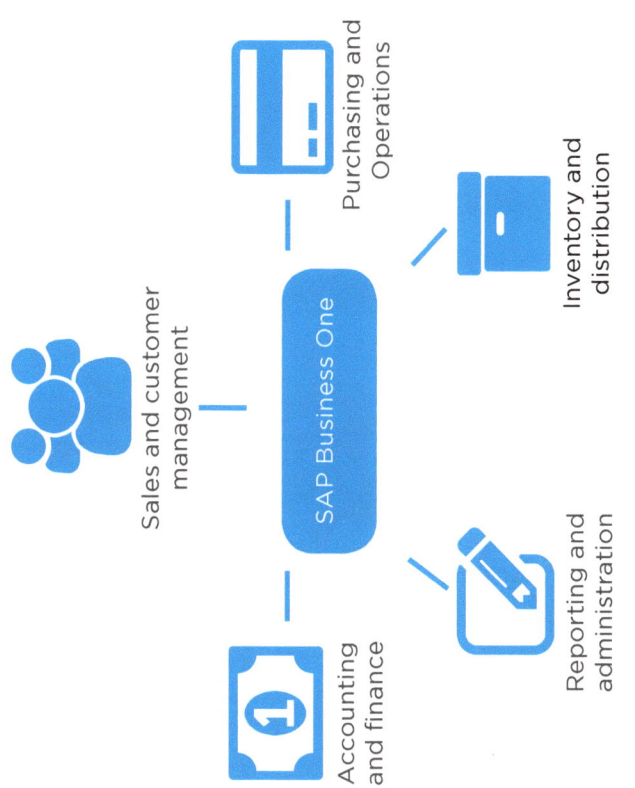

Sales and customer management

Accounting and finance

Purchasing and Operations

Inventory and distribution

SAP Business One

Reporting and administration

SAP Business One

QuickBooks vs. SAP Business One Cheat Sheet

QuickBooks vs. SAP Business One Cheat Sheet

You might be wondering how QuickBooks does when compared to SAP Business One? Reviewing some high-level functionality of SAP Business One reveals that QuickBooks may be holding back your growing business from achieving its business goals:

Area	QuickBooks	SAP Business One
Account Numbers	Optional account numbers but no segmentation for summary reporting and organizing your general ledger.	Up to 10 segments.
Inventory	Basic tracking through the addition of desktop and web based add-ons.	Inventory management: Lot tracking and serial numbers, Batches, Multi-warehouse support, FIFO, Average Cost, Standard Cost.
Scalability	Slows significantly as data size grows. No platform to move up to.	Scales with growth and can handle large databases. Supports transaction archiving.
Custom Reporting	Difficult to use and limited to the average user.	Based on industry leader Crystal Reports.
Flexibility	Minimal configurability and no user customizability.	Advanced user customizability features including unlimited user-defined tables, fields and objects capabilities.
Work Flow	Graphical flow chart on screen to help navigate.	Customizable automation features.
Security	Limited functional password security.	Deep functional and data ownership security.

Copyright Information

Vision33 Inc.

Vision33

Vision33 Incorporated

6 Hughes, Suite #220
Irvine, CA 92618
USA

www.vision33.com

For more information

http://www.vision33.com/products/sap-business-one

Vision33, the Vision33 brandmark, and any other product or service names or slogans contained in this document are property of Vision33, and their respective companies, may not be copied, imitated or used, in whole or in part, without the prior written permission of Vision33 Inc.

Complying with all applicable copyright laws is the responsibility of the user. Without limiting the rights under copyright, no part of this document may be reproduced, stored in or introduced into a retrieval system, or transmitted in any form or by any means (electronic, mechanical, photocopying, recording, or otherwise), or for any purpose, without the express written permission of Vision33.

SAP, the SAP logo, and the SAP partner logo are trademarks or registered trademarks of SAP AG in Germany and in several other countries all over the world.